MY FAMILY CHOSE ME

By Jasmine Pitt

Illustrated By Michael Farrar

My Family Chose Me by Jasmine Pitt

Text Copyright © 2020 Jasmine Pitt

Illustration Copyright © 2020 Michael Farrar

Formatting by Sanghamitra Dasgupta

All rights reserved

ISBN: 978-1-950861-31-6

Thank you for purchasing this book and complying with copyright laws by not reproducing, scanning or distributing any part of it in any form without permission.

Published by His Glory Creations Publishing, LLC

Wendell, North Carolina

Printed in the United States

"You were meant for us"

In loving memory of my adoptive parents

Thurman Lee Pitt & Cora Rebecca Pitt

(06/28/1926-01/02/2013)   (10/31/1947-01/02/2013)

Meet Jasmine Anderson, she is a seven-year-old girl who loves to spend time with her family.

They do all sorts of things together like camping, watch movies, and play games!

Everywhere their family went together, there were always questions! Lots of questions, especially about Jasmine. Some questions would be about her hair, freckles, how tiny she was, or if she was in their family or not. She thought it was all grown-up talk.

One day Jasmine went through all the stuff in her room, searching for something to take to school the next day for show and tell. After 30 minutes of no luck, she sat down in front of her mirror and began playing with a favorite pink and black-stuffed pig. She noticed that her hair was really big & very curly. No one else in her family had hair like hers.

She noticed that she had spots all over her face that her mom called freckles. She had just gotten them a year earlier and was still trying to figure them out. No one else in her family had freckles either.

She even noticed that she had the darkest skin complexion in her family. No one else in her family had skin as tan as hers. Jasmine sat thinking about all the family outings and how she was always the center of attention, everywhere she went. Maybe, it was her tan skin, or it could have been the freckles.

Later that day, her mom took her along with her brother and sister to the park to play. They were having a blast! While taking a break from playing, Jasmine overheard a lady sitting next to her mom and the lady asked, "Where did you get her from?" Jasmine was curious to hear her mom's answer. She was familiar with all kinds of questions such as why she had freckles or if she had known where she got her eyes from, but this question was always odd. It almost made her feel as if she was carried to her family by a stork like her older brother said. But her mom responded to the lady that she was "adopted."

Jasmine repeated the word over and over in her head. She knew she had to ask her mom what the word meant. She knew that she didn't quite look like everyone else in her family, but not everyone looks alike, but maybe that was a clue. That night before dinner, she looked over family photos to find hints to what her mom could have meant by "adopted." She was lost; she had no idea.

That night before dinner, Jasmine asked her mom & dad what the word "adopted " meant? They were shocked that she asked and Jasmine told them what she had overheard at the park earlier.

Her mom explained to her that when she was a baby, they decided to have a daughter. They met and fell in love with her so much that they wanted her to be a part of their family. They chose her as their daughter.

Her dad explained that when you become adopted in someone's family, you accept and love them for who they are. It didn't matter where they were born or how they looked, they are then considered family, no matter what.

That night, while sitting on her bed, Jasmine grasped her stuffed pig that her older brother had given her. She thought about how she noticed she looked much different from anyone in her family. It all made sense to her now, she was truly special. She had to be special to be chosen to be in her family.

The next day was show and tell at her school. This was something Jasmine was looking forward to since the first day of third grade. She thought about taking her stuffed pig to class, but had the perfect idea for what she would share with the class instead.

In the classroom walked Jasmine with a family photo in hand. She was excited for the bell to ring. She was excited to tell the class just how her family chose her to be a part of their family- well, her family now!

In the classroom walked Jasmine with a family photo in hand. She was excited for the bell to ring. She was excited to tell the class just how her family chose her to be a part of their family- well, her family now!

ABOUT THE AUTHOR

Jasmine Pitt is a mom of two with a bachelor's degree in Criminal Justice residing in the state of Maryland. She is employed at a pharmaceutical company that specializes in treating Cystic Fibrosis patients.

Jasmine is one of 3 biological siblings out of 6 that are adoptees. Her first book was inspired to help cultivate the conversation between parents and adoptee children about their particular family bond. Adoption is a subject that is dear to her heart. She believes it is important that parents share their extraordinary journey with their children on how they became one.

Connect with Jasmine

IG: jasminepittwrites
Twitter: JPittwrites
FB: authoressjasminepitt
Email: jasminepittwrites@gmail.com
Website: www.jasminepittwrites.com

His Glory Creations Publishing, LLC (HGCP) is an International Christian Book Publishing Company, which helps launch the creative works of new, aspiring and seasoned authors across the globe, through stories that are inspirational, empowering, life-changing or educational in nature, including poetry, journals, children's books, fiction and non-fiction works.

DESIRE TO KNOW MORE ABOUT HGCP?

Contact Information:

CEO/Founder: Felicia C. Lucas

www.hisglorycreationspublishing.com

Facebook: His Glory Creations Publishing

Email: hgcpublishingllc@gmail.com

Phone: 919-679-1706